STATEMENT OF THE CLAIM

OF

THE STATE OF ALABAMA

AGAINST

THE UNITED STATES.

GIDEON & CO., PRINTERS, WASHINGTON, D. C.

STATEMENT OF THE CLAIM

OF

THE STATE OF ALABAMA

AGAINST

THE UNITED STATES;

WITH

ARGUMENT IN SUPPORT THEREOF, AND NUMEROUS PRECEDENTS FROM USAGE OF THE GOVERNMENT, AND CASES IN POINT,

NOW BEFORE CONGRESS.

WASHINGTON:
GIDEON & CO., PRINTERS.
1850

SYNOPSIS OF CONTENTS.

Exhibits.

GENERAL STATEMENT

OF

THE CLAIM OF THE STATE OF ALABAMA

ON

THE UNITED STATES.

By the 3d clause of the 6th section of the compact made with the State of Alabama on her admission into the Union, 2d March, 1819, it is stipulated, "that five per cent. of the nett proceeds of the lands lying within the said territory, and which shall be sold by Congress, from and after the 1st day of September in the year 1819, after deducting all expenses incident to the same, shall be reserved" for internal improvements, "of which three-fifths shall be applied under direction of the legislature thereof, (the State) and two-fifths under the direction of Congress."

By the 3d section of the act of 3d May, 1822, it is enacted, "that the Secretary of the Treasury shall from time to time, and whenever the quarterly accounts of public moneys of the several land offices in the State of Alabama, shall be settled, pay three per cent. of the nett proceeds of the sales of the lands of the United States lying within the State of Alabama," &c., "to such person or persons as may or shall be authorized by the legislature of the State of Alabama to receive the same."

A subsequent act surrendered the two per cent. fund also to the State.

Under the foregoing stipulation and provision, the U. S. made several adjustments of the accounts of lands sold in Alabama, and from time to time allotted to the State certain sums alleged to be the full amount due to the State. In 1848 the State had reason to distrust the accuracy of these settlements, and her Legislature passed an act for the appointment of an agent to revise them. On this revision at the Treasury Department, it was ascertained and admitted that $103,991 20, which had accrued to the State between the years 1820 and 1831, had not been paid, though unquestionably due; and this sum was therefore paid in January last.

The State, pursuant to a late act of her legislature, now claims interest on this deferred payment. Freely admitting that, as a general rule, the United States are not liable to interest, and ought not to pay it, yet the State, in common with all the officers of the Government, and every Congress since '76, is also aware that there are exceptions to the rule. It is undeniable that cases occur in which principle and usage demand the payment of interest by the United States as the due measure of justice. Numerous precedents exist of this practice.

Alabama claims that hers is a case of this peculiarity. She asks but that, which is strictly just. Although injured by detention of moneys, which were hers by purchase and payment of consideration, yet she would silently submit to the loss, did she not also feel it right that she should appeal to national justice. To it she does appeal, not for a favor, but a *right;* a right, if purchase and payment on the one hand, withholding and injury on the other, combined with precedent, principle, and the highest usages of the country, *can* create a right against a power which is liable only through the spontaneous action of her own representatives.

Exhibit "A" sets out the particulars and arithmetical data of the claim. Should it, however, fail to receive the anticipated recognition of Congress, then the State presents another, and entirely distinct claim; one which she would not advance but in case of the denial of her prior claim. This secondary one *none will contest.* It is merely for *re*payment to the State of moneys which she overpaid to the United States, through the error of the latter; moneys which she did not owe, and which are in truth her property in the United States' treasury. The particulars of this matter are given in exhibit B.

With this brief outline of the claim under consideration, we proceed to its statement "in extenso" in the following argument.

ARGUMENT

The claim of Alabama, seeking a just compensation for wrong and injury, may at first seem a matter of exclusive interest to herself; but it will soon appear that in asserting her own rights she advocates, also, a great principle for all the States, but especially for those who, like her, have compacts with the United States containing mutual stipulations. Her claim presents grave questions. It involves the consideration of the extent of *practical* obligation imposed on the United States by their own compact; whether they may leave *their* covenants unperformed; and if unperformed, and injury results, whether the injured State is to receive any, and what compensation.

The claim of Alabama arises under the compact of March 2, 1819, made upon her admission into the Union. It contains the provisions common to new States. Among these are the mutual stipulations, which had their being in the early policy of the United States. This policy was suggested by the condition of the country at that day. The Federal Government found itself possessed of a vast, and, except by the Indian, an unpeopled territory. To encourage settlement on the public lands, to swell the treasury by their sale, and to build up new States, was deemed a wise policy. As territories passed into States, and as star after star was added to the Union, public burthens decreased, and an additional pillar was placed under the common fabric.

Hence arose the policy found in the admission compacts of nearly all the new States, commencing with Ohio, in 1802. This policy consisted in something to be done by the State on the one side, and the United States on the other. The State was to surrender to the United States all waste lands, and to abstain from taxing public lands for 5 years after their sale.

As an equivalent therefor, the United States were to pay the State 5 per cent. of the nett proceeds of land sales, for roads and other improvements—three-fifths to be expended by the State, and two-fifths by the General Government. In some instances, the whole 5 per cent. was under the control of the State.

The exemption from taxation for 5 years, and the pledge of one-twentieth of his purchase money to the making of improvements in his

State, induced the emigrant to purchase, while the State's per centage stimulated her also to promote the sales of public land.

The wisdom of this policy is best commended by its success. It is continued to this day; and out of 245 millions of acres of public lands, $94,571,339 have passed into the public treasury since the origin of the land system.

These mutual stipulations were obviously the *equivalents* for each other. The United States swelled her treasury at the cost of the State, but agreed to compensate her by a per centage. On the other hand, the State was enriched by this pledge of one-twentieth of the proceeds of land sales; but it was no gratuity; she *purchased* it, and dearly too. Taxation is the highest attribute of sovereignty. Its exercise is necessary to State existence; and in waiving it, the *State paid just that amount of bonus to promote the sales of public lands.*

For the performance of the covenants of the United States, no security was given but that of their pledged faith. Nothing, however, was left to the faith of *the State.* Due performance by her was secured beyond the possibility of hazard. The prohibition of taxation, when assented to by Alabama, was an impassable barrier to its exercise. An attempt to tax earlier could not be enforced. But on the United States no such iron compulsion rested. *Good faith* was the only guarantee given to the State, and Alabama now cites that faith to respond to her appeal in the Congress of the Nation.

The claim to this good faith is greatly strengthened by the fact that the 'five years" of non-taxation (as stipulated in the compact) was unexpectedly swelled to a period ranging from 10 to 17. This extraordinary enlargement arose from the old system of sales. Lands were then sold on a credit—$\frac{1}{4}$ paid down, the balance in 2, 3, and 4 years, with interest, and a year's grace was then added. Mean while the purchaser went into possession, but he did not get his patent, nor was the land deemed to "be sold," until full and final payment of his purchase money was made. The United States claimed, and enforced the claim, that the 5 years of non-taxation did not commence till then. If a State taxed earlier than five years after the purchaser's final payment, and sold for non-payment, the land office invariably refused to recognise the title of the tax-purchaser, and even to accept from him, as a mere tax-purchaser, the balance of purchase money. This doctrine and practice are set forth in Attorney General Wirt's opinion, and Commissioner Meig's report. (See exhibit, "C.")

Not one out of a hundred purchasers paid regularly. A great mass of overdue balances gradually accrued, and finally *relief laws* were enacted, extending the time of payment from 1809, year by year, to 1821. Then by other measures purchases were kept alive, so that the balances did not expire until 1831.

During this period, from the first relief law in 1809, to their expiration in 1831, large quantities of *settled* land in the fund States were deemed to be "*not sold*" until 1831, and on them the 5 years of non-taxation commenced to run only in that year. Yet all these lands had been settled and improved prior to 1820, and some of them 10 years earlier. In fact it is impossible to state with exactness the length to which the taxation limit enlarged itself. All that *can* be said is, that on all credit sales in Alabama, the actual taxation limit was not less than 10, nor more than 17 years.

This unexpected and most serious addition to the State's part of the compact adds powerful weight to the claim, she otherwise has, for the prompt performance by the United States of the *compensating covenant*.

Having thus introduced the origin and nature of these compacts between the Federal Government and the fund States, and having exhibited the respective positions of the parties, it is proper next to inquire to what extent the United States have performed *their* covenants.

The facts—facts of record—compel the assertion that the United States have been in default, in continued and unjustifiable default, to most, if not to all, the fund States. They postponed their per centage; and when paid, the amount was not the true sum. For many years, the moneys due to States were retained in, and enriched the National Treasury. Errors of singular uniformity in favor of the United States, and against the States, characterize their ex parte accounts of this fund; and, finally, a true settlement was attained by the States only through an expensive agency.

These remarks apply with most force to the early days of the Government. In modern times, it is cheerfully conceded that the departmental officers have been, and now are, faithful and accurate in their accounts. But the evidence of facts justifies the charge that has been alleged. Within the last four years, five of the fund States appointed agents to revise their accounts. Four of these accounts have been fully restated, and one of them partially. Each restatement disclosed the same facts and the same result. Error was in every account. Just credits had been withheld, and balances were found due to all, to wit:

To Ohio,	$65,749 09	
To Indiana,	49,522 70	
To Illinois,	26,025 63	
To Mississippi,	2,576 89	(partial statement only)
To Alabama,	103,991 20	

In the case of Alabama, the last of these revisions, a very serious fact respecting all these accounts was first ascertained and admitted. *It was the entire omission of a large item of the proceeds of sales.* Its magnitude may be inferred from the fact, that in the case of Alabama it amounted to $2,131,105 06. The proceeds thus omitted were payments made under the Relief laws. When the price of land was reduced from $2 to $1 25 per acre, purchase moneys that had previously become forfeited on account of failure of full payment, were in many cases restored, to enable the purchase to be completed at the reduced rate. The purchaser was also empowered to relinquish one or more tracts of land, on which partial payments had been made, and to apply these payments to complete the purchase money on a tract retained. The payments thus made, by restored forfeitures and relinquishments, were wholly withheld from the account of sales; and although many millions of acres in the several States were paid for with moneys from these sources, the States received no per centage thereon. They were not even aware of such proceeds, until the Alabama agency discovered and disclosed the fact. In consequence of it, Ohio, Indiana, Illinois, and Mississippi have again restated, or are now restating, their accounts, to add to their former balance the sums which are also their due under the discoveries of Alabama. *She* is therefore entitled to the consideration of her sister States for the establishment of this common right.

The error that omitted these proceeds receives strong comment in the fact, that out of four departments of the Government which had jurisdiction of the Alabama principles,* not one officer questioned the propriety of inserting them.

These grave facts, perpetuated on the Government records, sustain the allegation of default on the part of the United States in the performance of their fund obligations. And is there excuse for this failure to render the just account that is now acknowledged? The United States possessed all the requisites for a fair adjustment: lands, sales, officers, books, were all their own. Complexity there was none. A simpler matter of account cannot be proposed! Why, then, has the

---

*** The Land Office, Secretary of Interior, Attorney General, and 1st Comptroller.**

creation of an expensive agency been necessary to the attainment of justice by the States? This pregnant fact, taken in connexion with the uniformity of error in favor of the United States, naturally suggests the inquiry whether there be any, and what, remedy for these many wrongs.

Before proceeding to this consideration, however, we will recapitulate our argument thus far.

We have shown—

1st. The origin of the "fund" compact, to wit, in the policy to promote the sale of public lands.

2d. That the 5 *per cent. fund* and the *non-taxation* were the equivalents for each other.

3d. That the compact, assented to by the State, effectually secured the performance of the non-taxation stipulation.

4th. That the United States so construed their land laws as to extend the five years of non-taxation to a period ranging from ten to seventeen years.

5th. That the States had no security from the United States other than their plighted faith for the performance of the compact on their part.

6th. That the claim of the State to this fund was enhanced by the unexpected and serious extension of the non-taxation period.

7th. That the United States had the adjustment of the account entirely to themselves.

8th. That the keeping of the fund account was a simple task: that palpable errors existed therein; among which was the entire omission of one distinct class of proceeds, amounting, in Alabama alone, to over two millions of dollars.

9th. That the facts sustain a case of grave and inexcusable default on the part of the United States.

It will be observed that the foregoing remarks are justified by admitted facts. The charge which they sustain is, the stating of erroneous accounts, and the omission therein of appropriate items. To this charge is now to be added another, and, if possible, a greater one, to wit, *the withholding for many years the sums which their own accounts showed to be due to the State.*

The compact with Alabama entitled her to an expenditure of 5 per cent. in improvements for her benefit—three-fifths at her own discretion, and two-fifths by the United States. The meaning of the compact clearly is, that the payments shall be made *immediately*—as fast as moneys for land sales come into the Treasury. The language of the compact is, "that 5 per cent. *of* the nett proceeds shall be reserved," &c., not 5 per cent. *out* of the proceeds, or arising from them, but an actual hypothecation of one-twentieth of the original proceeds themselves. This language contemplated an immediate ownership in, and of course an *immediate use of*, the fund as soon as it could conveniently be paid over. That it was so understood by the parties, is evident from the provision made by law for executing it. In May, 1822, an act executory of the compacts with Alabama and other fund States was passed, directing the Secretary of the Treasury "from time to time, *whenever the quarterly accounts of public moneys of the several land offices should be settled*," to pay the 3 per cent. Therefore, in order to *faithfully* perform the compact, *prompt* payment was requisite. Mere payment at some undefined future time would not satisfy it; nor would any thing short of actual payment on *the quarterly adjustment of the accounts.*

This was also just on general principles. If the 5 per cent. was really to be an equivalent or substitute for taxation, *its time of payment ought to take the place of the tax*, thus to aid the State, when her treasury was deprived of its legitimate resource by taxation.

Every settlement on public lands brought with it increased burdens to the State. The new settler and his family swelled the population which claimed the protection of the State. In proportion to the population must be the domestic representation, the judiciary, police, roads, &c., and other incidents to society. All these are charges on the State. Her resources lie in *taxation*. When this right is unfettered, she can easily provide for her wants by an equable taxation on property. The increase of population, in this case, does not augment the public burdens, because the new settler tenders for taxation his new home. He brings with him the elements of a self-discharge of the cost which attaches to his citizenship. In such a case, all is well; but in that of *taxation fettered*, as in the case under consideration, the equilibrium is lost, and the State must look elsewhere for relief from the burdens of an increasing population. The compact professes to substitute for taxation 5 per cent. of the settler's payment; but it is no substitute, if susceptible of indefinite delay. Prompt payment—payment *at the very time* when the settler augments the public burdens, and when his property, otherwise taxable, is exempt under the contract, is the very essence and soul of its stipulations.

Thus sound principle concurs with the compact and with the law of 1822 in establishing immediate payment as one of the requisites called for by a faithful performance of the compact.

Besides this, however, mere payment does not satisfy an obligation, unless made on the day when due. Money is more valuable to a party at some periods than at others. In early years, the State's means are small. She has much to do, and all to be done at once. Then her moneys are most beneficial, and the withholding of them the most injurious; and if wilfully withheld by an able debtor, she is fairly entitled to compensation, as the measure of the damage sustained by the detention, and of the benefit derived by the debtor from the use of her money.

Let us apply these principles to the case of Alabama. It has been seen that there was error and wrong, in respect to her three per cent.—the portion payable to the State. Do we find, in the performance of the two per cent. branch of the compact, any thing to redeem the evils of the other? Far from it. On the contrary, *there* the wrong is even deeper—the evil yet greater. The United States agreed to expend the two per cent. fund, and to do so as fast as received at the treasury. Yet for twenty-two years that fund lay in their treasury, unexpended, save for the United States wants; and these the years of Alabama's greatest need of commercial facilities and her smallest means for their construction! Though error existed in the three per cent. account, a part of *it* was paid, *but not a dollar of the two per cent.*, until 1841 and 1842. Its amount, as then adjusted at the Treasury, was $238,405.21. This large sum, *purchased* by Alabama for a specific use *by her lost taxation*, had up to this period only enriched the United States.

It might be here asked, ought not the United States to render compensation for this withholding of a trust fund from the cestui que trust? but Alabama desires to prefer no claim that is not well assured by the highest principles of justice. She therefore passes by this item, waiving any claim upon it, and alluding to it only as proof of the serious default of the United States in the *time* of payment of *acknowledged dues*.

The claim she presents is limited to that portion of her purchased fund which was found due to her by the late restatement of her account in the Treasury Department, and paid in January last. It arose from introducing into the account the previously omitted payments for lands made by restored forfeitures and relinquishments. Their gross sum exceeded two millions of dollars. The State's per centage on it was $103,991 20. She now claims interest on the deferred payment of this balance. For statement thereof see exhibit A. The precise amount of each payment, with the date of accrual to the State, are set out distinctly in the restated account. One-half accrued in 1821, and the other half between that and 1831—an average period of twenty-five years. During these twenty-five years, Alabama often demanded of the United States her dues from this fund. Not receiving them, and unable to postpone her public improvements, she was finally coerced to raise the means by the issue of State bonds, bearing interest. The fact of her wants is thus evidenced. Mean while her *non taxation* stipulation was extended from five to ten years, and in most instances to seventeen. Her waste lands passed to the United States, and she herself was held to the very letter of strict performance. And to crown the whole, is the fact that the United States, becoming possessed of the bonds of Alabama, issued in 1836, to the amount of one million six hundred and ninety-seven thousand dollars, which bonds were issued (in part) in consequence of the United States' default, have invariably demanded and enforced the prompt payment of semi-annual interest thereon, from their issue to this day. *Yet during all this time the United States were in fact the debtor, and Alabama the creditor,* to a certain extent.

This is a very important consideration. It alone is deemed to be decisive for the present claim. Let us look at the facts, and apply to them the common and indisputable rules of all dealing. In 1836, the United States became possessed of certain bonds of Alabama, and have ever since received interest on them at six per cent. But in 1836, and for many years prior, the United States owed Alabama $103,991 20, (in round terms $104,000.) Consequently, Alabama was entitled, in 1836, to have that sum endorsed on the bonds, and thereby to have so much of the principal absolutely and forever discharged.

The account on these bonds would then have stood thus:

Total amount of bonds - - - - -	$1,697,000
Less by amount due Alabama, say - - -	104,000
Balance due, and on which Alabama is to pay interest,	$1,593,000

By the error of the United States this indisputable credit was not given; and in consequence Alabama was wrongfully held to pay interest on the face amount of her bonds, and has been thus held to pay from 1836 to the present time. Consequently, she has overpaid the legal interest by paying interest on this $104,000, which she did not owe. The semi-annual interest on that sum, at six per cent., is $3,120. Each payment thereof was wrong. Twenty-eight of them have been made. In a schedule hereto attached, marked exhibit B, is contained the account of these illegal overpayments.

If, therefore, the United States should repudiate altogether the payment of interest upon the balance due the State, yet here is another wholly distinct ground of claim by Alabama—*it is to get back moneys wrongfully overpaid by her to the United States.*

But it is contended that every good principle, and the usage of the United States, entitle her to interest on the $104,000 for the entire period of its being due.

The United States *always* charge interest upon indebtedness, as an indispensable element of account. They have so charged Alabama and the other fund States; and, when the latter owed interest on their bonds in the United States' possession, the United States not only charged interest, but actually applied the State's per centage to discharge the interest; and that, too, although the per centage was not an open sum, but a *trust fund,* pledged to a specific use, and one in which every State in the Union had an interest and title, as well as the indebted State.

Let these rules work both ways. As the United States charged Alabama interest on a *presumed* indebtedness, why should not they in turn pay *her* interest on an *actual* one?

As the United States charge the fund States interest, and detain their per centage to pay it, why should not the United States in turn pay interest on their per centage *when wrongfully detained?*

When Alabama paid interest wrongfully, on money she did not owe, why should not the wrong be made right by the United States returning the money wrongfully received?

To answer these questions otherwise than affirmatively would be to sink the sovereignty of the States in that of the United States; for the United States cannot escape from the force of these established rules, except under the plea of the prerogative of sovereignty. Are the States less sovereign, or less seized of rights, than the United States, the creature and representative of them all? Nay! It is *they* that are the *real* sovereigns, and the actual source of political life and power in the United States.

And why should not the United States pay, and Alabama receive interest? Her right to the *principal* was conceded, and it has been paid. Her right to it twenty-five years ago has also been conceded. Her demand of it, the injury inflicted upon her by its detention, the errors of the United States, and their use of her money, are all alike unquestioned. Why, then, should not interest be paid? Interest is at once the measure of, and compensation for, the damage; the equivalent to the one party for detention, paid by the other for the use of money.

Why, then, should it not be paid? Is it that its payment, in this case, would conflict with the practice of the Government? We will examine the subject, and prove that, so far from conflicting, it would be in strict conformity with its theory and practice under every administration.

The payment of interest by the United States has been often discussed, and has recently undergone so thorough an investigation, that it is unnecessary here to go into the subject at large. A few cases will be given, and remarks made upon them, to show that the case of Alabama comes well within the rules which sustain the payment of interest, and is distinguished by strong characteristics from those cases which are without them.

The great bulk of opinion and decision respecting the payment of interest by the United States has been given under circumstances not applicable to the present case. Nearly all relate to the allowance of interest by *the Departments or Executive officers*. It is *their* power that is chiefly examined, and *their* allowance of interest that is canvassed and censured. Congress may be jealous of the exercise of so dangerous a power by merely Executive officers, but Alabama seeks Congressional, and not Departmental action.

Another marked distinction between this and ordinary cases is the fact, that the latter are the claims of individuals, unknown to the Government until presented, vouched, and allowed. They then, for the first time, become a debt against the United States.

The case of Alabama is in strong distinction. It is the claim of an equal and a sovereign. It arises under a treaty compact, (for these compacts are in the nature of treaties, and are entitled to the usages appurtenant to compacts between sovereignties.) Its existence is made known by the treaty. It is secured by law. It begins where the other class of claims ends, being founded on a debt against the United States, under a compact, and a law executory of it. The United States are bound to take notice of it, and to provide for its due payment as for any other national obligation, even without special demand. It is a question of right arising from a compact, and not an original demand. Therefore rules, properly applicable to individual cases, fail to reach this. Nothing is in common to the two, except that both are called by the common name of "claims."

The general rule applicable to claims may be gathered from the opinion of Attorney General Taney, in Major Thorpe's case, (p. 841.) (Attorney General's opinion.) Its substance is that there is no legal or constitutional objection to the allowance of interest by Executive officers "*if justly due*," but that the cases are rare in which interest *can be* "justly due," the United States being presumed to be always ready to pay. (For this opinion see exhibit D.)

It follows that the converse of the proposition in this opinion must be equally true, and therefore that there *may be* claims where interest is "justly due," and that the officers ought to pay interest on them. By referring to the opinion, it will be seen that this conclusion is inevitable from its reasoning, and that this class of cases are those in which the claim in proper shape is before the Government, and delay of payment is caused by the default of the United States.

The test upon which the exemption of the United States from interest is made to depend is the fact—which of the parties delayed the payment of the principal? Who was in default? In the case under consideration, Mr. Taney reasons thus: The accounting officers are not forbid to pay interest, if it is "justly due." But the United States are always ready to pay, when a claim in proper shape is before them; *therefore* it can rarely happen that they are "justly chargeable with interest." Why? Because it is the fault of the claimant, says the opinion. Hence, then, it is the *fault* that decides the justice of an interest demand.

When, therefore, the United States *are* in fault; when the claim, in proper shape, *is* before them, and that the delay of payment is theirs, the case is one of those "rare" occurrences, which the Attorney General deemed possible, though not likely, where the United States are "justly chargeable with interest;" and it becomes a subject of demand so just, that even the accounting officers might pay it.

It scarcely needs to be remarked, that the case of Alabama is precisely one of those rare exceptions. Demand for her due, apart from special demand, was always before the Government, under the obligations of a treaty compact, and the provisions of an executory law. This continued notice and demand rendered any non-payment a clear case of laches. The United States themselves admit the perpetual obligation of this demand, by making adjustments and payments from year to year of the per centage, without special demand.

The claim is therefore one which, in the opinion of Chief Justice

Taney, even the accounting officers ought to pay; and if so, then, *a fortiori*, is Congress bound to pay it.

We will now consider another case.

On page 542, Attorney General's opinions, is found an opinion of Mr. Wirt on certain reciprocal rights and duties of the Government and the States. It was given on the claim of Virginia foi interest, under an act of Congress which guarantied payment of her expenses during the war with Great Britain, with interest. His reasoning is, that where the United States fail to do a thing, to the performance of which they are bound, and the State does it from necessity, and obtains the means by borrowing on interest, the United States are bound to make the State good, in principal and interest.

Here, again, Alabama presents a case of entire analogy. The United States were bound to pay her moneys for internal improvements. They failed to do so. The improvements were indispensable to the State. The want of commercial facilities were as fatal to her interests as the presence of an invading enemy to Virginia. She was therefore compelled to make the improvements in self defence. She borrowed money for the purpose, and paid interest for its use. According to Mr. Wirt, then, "the United States having failed to make such provision, and the State having to defend itself" (make the improvement) "by means of her own resources, the expenditure thus incurred forms a debt against the United States which they are bound to reimburse;" and as "the State has been obliged to borrow," "and pay interest, such debt is essentially a debt due by the United States, and both the principal and interest are to be paid by the United States."

We next invite attention to a remarkable case, in which the United States interwove in the code of her own polity, and of national usage, the principle that the payment of interest was indispensable to the just satisfaction of an acknowledged debt, under circumstances and reasoning of striking applicability to the present case.

The case cited is found in Mr. Wirt's opinion (page 560) on the convention of St. Petersburgh. This was an award by the Emperor of Russia on certain questions between England and the United States, arising out of the war of 1812. It awarded "just indemnification" to the United States for slaves and property carried away during the war. The question was, whether the "*just indemnification*" included *interest* as well as principal; or whether the indemnity stopped at the naked value of the property. The British commissioner contended against interest. Mr. Wirt reasons thus:

"A wrong must be repaired in whole, if it would be indemnified; that a reparation of $\frac{1}{2}$ or $\frac{3}{4}$ would not be enough; that the taking away the property originally was wrong, and the continuance of the possession of the property was an additional wrong; that the property was detained 11 years in violation of a treaty; that it is not consistent with the usage of nations to redress wrong by a mere return of the naked value, without interest, even of belligerent nations, far less of friendly powers;" and he concludes by deciding that interest is a necessary part of the indemnity.

The facts of this case are substantially those of Alabama; and the reasoning of Mr. Wirt applies with unanswerable strength. There was a treaty compact between the United States and Great Britain; so between the United States and Alabama. Great Britain violated the one, the United States the other; one by commission, the other by omission. The one did what she ought not to have done, (take property;) the other left undone what they ought to have done, (pay money.) In both cases there was equal transgression. The United States claimed to be made whole by Great Britain; Alabama now claims the same of the United States. The original act of Great Britain was decided by the award of the Emperor of Russia to be a wrong committed in 1815. The original act of the United States was decided by her own officers, in their official capacity, to be a wrong committed in 1821. Great Britain and the United States both admit the wrong, and offer reparation by payment of the naked value at the perpetration of the wrong —*i. e.*, the principal. But Mr. Wirt says the *detaining* was an equal wrong with the original act; that the parties lost the use of their property, and that the only proper indemnity is reparation for the *whole* of it, —for the original and the *continuing* wrong—and that interest is a necessary part of the indemnification under the law of nations. Accordingly, the United States demanded interest of Great Britain, and finally enforced it—enforced it as the due measure of national redress of wrong, as established by usage and principle. And such measure of redress Alabama confidently expects to receive from the United States. It is not to be believed that the United States will now *reverse* great national principles for which they successfully contended, because of their own *reversed position* from *creditor* to *debtor*. Were the United States to reverse a great principle thus solemnly and conspicuously settled, and to reverse it here, where its rule is against them, such antagonist action would necessarily impair confidence in the faith of the Government, and destroy that fixity which is so essential in the principles and procedure of Government.

The foregoing cases show, that the claim of Alabama for interest is well sustained by the principles and usage of our Government.

We will now adduce another class of cases to show what has been the action of *Congress.*

As might be expected from a body possessing the power, almost unlimited, over claims, its action will be found more liberal than that of mere Executive officers. Liberality, generosity, and an enlarged equity, no less than strict justice, characterize their acts.

The cases cited will be those only in which interest has been paid as the due measure of relief.

1st. Where money is the basis of relief, interest is added as a part of the remedy.

Smith and Gates had purchased lands of the U. S. Title proved defective. Principal and interest were allowed. (U. S. S., vol. 6, p. 72.)

Joshua Sands, collector, was sued for vessel seized; he claimed for damages of the U. S.; he was allowed interest and costs. (Vol. 6, U. S. S., p. 150.)

John Thompson; interest allowed on money advanced, and also on services. (Vol. 6, p. 208.)

William Tharpe; interest allowed on claim for services and bill of charges. (Vol. 6, p. 476.)

Thomas Richardson, a suttler, to protect himself, he took out letters of administration, to soldiers who owed him. Repaid *with interest,* to extent of funds due to soldiers. (Vol. 6, p. 558.)

Marius G. Gilbert; the same. (Vol 6, p. 621.)

2d. In cases of accounts with the U. S., and also where a balance is found against the U. S., Congress pays interest. (Such is the case of Alabama.)

In 1802, *Arthur St. Clair;* his accounts referred to accounting officers, and balance paid with interest. (Vol. 6, p. 16.)

Stephen Sayre, 1807; his acc't settled and interest allowed. (Vol. 6, p. 65.)

T. Barclay, 1808. The same. (Vol. 6, p. 72.)

Wm. Baynham, 1810. The same. (Vol. 6, p. 89.)

Moses Young, 1810. The same. (Vol. 6, p. 89.)

J. Wheaton, 1806; balance due him by award, $1,600; interest from 1807, added. (Vol. 6, p. 166.)

R. Hills, 1819; account settled and interest paid. (Vol. 6, p. 231.)

Wm. Otis, 1829. The same. (Vol. 6, p. 396.)

3d. In case of unjustified detention of *property* by the U. S., Congress pays interest to compensate for the detention. *A fortiori*, is interest due for detention of *money*, it being always the subject of interest, but property rarely.

John Coles, 1802; vessel detained at Gibraltar by American consul; damages and *interest* paid. (Vol. 6, p. 51.)

D. Colton, 1809; vessel detained; damages and interest paid. (Vol. 6, p. 80.)

4th. Interest is a necessary part of *indemnity*.

N. Green, indemnified in a certain sum, and interest paid. (Vol. 6, p. 9, 28.)

5th. When the claim is founded on an equivalent rendered to the U. S., and the U. S. have received value therefor, they will pay the claim with interest, even though it be barred by a contract fully performed.

Congress disregards every barrier to a compensation which is just in principle. (See case of John Steinman and others.)

Steinman and others, in 1813, manufactured arms for the U. S., under a contract accompanied by a specimen. They delivered the arms and were paid the stipulated price. In 1826, they petitioned Congress for an additional allowance, because the arms were better than was required by the contract; also, because the Government had paid other contractors a higher price for same kind of articles under contracts.

Of course, these petitioners had no pretence of *right* on which to found their claim. They had made their contract and received the stipulated price. 13 years passed away since the transaction was concluded. It rested entirely on *equitable principles*. But Congress entertained the claim, and passed an act, not only giving them the increased rate, but also *interest* on it from 1813. (See vol. 6, U. S. S., p. 345.)

The cases last cited embrace the cardinal points of the Alabama claim. It, like them, is for interest. The basis of it (like point 1st) is *money;* like point 2d, it is a balance on account stated with the United States; like point 3d, it is a detention by the United States, but of *money* instead of *property;* like point 4th, interest is necessary to indemnify the State for injury and for interest paid by the State; and, like point 5th, the claim is founded on an ample equivalent rendered by her to the United States by the surrender of taxation.

The comparison of the cases of Stienman and Alabama is this: both rendered value to the United States under contracts; to *Stienman* the United States performed in full; to *Alabama* they failed. *Stienman* bargained with his eyes open, and a sample in his hand, was paid his price in full, and acquiesced for thirteen years; yet Congress overlooked all but the original value, increased the price, and added interest to boot. In the case of Alabama, no contract bars her. True, a contract there is, but *it* throws its heavy weight in her favor, and not against her.

We shall now cite a class of cases in which the United States have invariably paid interest to the States, as the "just compensation" for their performance of acts which it was the duty of the United States to do. This legislative action *practically* illustrates and sustains the principles laid down by Mr. Wirt in the case of Virginia, and quoted on page It conclusively establishes the principle that, in all cases of suitable emergency, the States may discharge duties which of right pertain to the United States alone, but which they omit through laches or necessity.

But it shows more. It establishes, also, the principle contended for, that the States, as sovereigns in themselves, and component parts of the common sovereignty representing their Union, stand on a platform of equality when respectively dealing with the united body; that prerogatives, which attach to sovereignties in their intercourse with individuals, are lost in the co-extensive privileges of the equal. Accordingly, we find that, in the accounts of the latter class, the ordinary rule, that governs adjustments between individuals, prevails. In their cases—the cases of equals—interest, unless waived by law or contract, attaches to non-payment, as an indispensable consequence. In a 2d class of cases—that of sovereigns and individuals—the equality of condition is lost, and with it the rule also. But in the 3d class the equality is restored, and with it the rule is again established.

And still more, this legislation, in connexion with the preceding cases, shows how vast the field is, from which spring the elements of demand for interest, as the due measure of satisfaction for the honor and faith of the United States. They exhibit the extent of exception to the rule, generally deemed so fixed, that the United States never pay interest, and prove that, like every rule, it has its just exceptions.

March 3, 1825, vol. 4, U. S. S., page 132.—Interest to Virginia on expenditures for the United States during the war of 1812.

May 13, 1826, vol. 4, U. S. S., page 161.—The same to Maryland.

May 20, 1826, vol. 4, page 175.—The same to Delaware.

May 20, 1826, vol. 4, page 177.—The same to Baltimore.

May 22, 1826, vol. 4, page 193.—The same to New York.

March 3, 1827, vol. 4, page 240.—The same to Pennsylvania.

March 22, 1832.—The same to South Carolina.

In addition to these cases, are two in which the present Senate passed bills giving interest to Georgia and Maine.

A large mass of precedent has now been shown in every department of the Government, all concurring in a common principle. The opinions of Attorney Generals Wirt and Taney, the practice of the Government in its foreign and domestic relations, the legislation of Congress, and the dealings with the States of the Union, harmonize in establishing that the State of Alabama is entitled to interest in a case so analogous to the numerous instances cited.

It only remains to be seen what the law of nations, and the policy of our own laws suggest as applicable to the case. But two authorities will be cited. Let them speak for themselves.

Vattel says: "All the promises, the conventions, all the contracts of the sovereign, are naturally subjected to the same rules as those of private persons."—(Vattel, lib. 2, chap. 14, p. 213.)

The eminent jurist, *Justice Story*, says, in Thorndike vs. United States, (1 Mason's Rep., 20:) "If the present were a contract between private citizens, there can be no doubt that the court would be bound to give interest upon the contract up to the time of payment; and if by law the amount due on the contract could be pleaded as a tender or a set-off to a private debt, it would be a good bar in the full extent of the principal and interest due at the time of such tender or set-off. Nay, more: if the note or promise were made by a citizen to the Government, the latter might enforce its claim to the like extent. Can it make any difference in the construction of the contract that the Government is the *debtor*, instead of the *creditor?* In reason, in justice, in equity, it ought to make none, and there is not a scintilla of law to justify any. If a suit could be maintained against the Government, I do not perceive why it would not be as much the duty of the court to render judgment in such suit for the principal and interest, in the same manner, and to the same extent, as it would in the case of private citizens. The United States have no prerogative to claim one law upon their own contracts as *creditors*, another as *debtors*. If *as creditors* they are entitled to interest; *as debtors*, they are bound also to pay it."

The force and propriety of this reasoning must strike every one. Were the United States then to refuse interest to Alabama, they would do that for which Mr. Justice Story says "they have no prerogative," and far less have they law. As creditors enforcing interest from Great Britain under treaty, and from the States under contract; but as debtors refusing to pay it, though their debt is admitted, and the instruments are the same, what would it be but to assume, under the iron hand of power, the position for which the great jurist expressly declares there is neither law nor prerogative?

Such action by the United States cannot be contemplated. A dignified and honorable nation, it only needs to know the right, to do it; and in their dealing with Alabama, they will doubtless conclude, when they know the facts, that in the jurist's words, "as creditors they have taken interest of the State, as debtors they are bound also to pay it."

To close this branch of the argument, it only remains to notice the contrast between this and a recent case, the subject of much discussion.

The *Galphin claim* was originally against the Indians—then against Great Britain—next against Georgia; but, in the opinion of its opponents, never a just one against the United States. It did not originate against them; and if it lay against them at all, it was only by implication. Thus the first great element necessary for an interest claim was here *uncertain*, i. e., the actual right of claimant to the principal from the United States.

Greater contrast cannot exist than does exist, in the foregoing respects, between the Galphin and the Alabama claims. The latter arises from a contract with the United States—is the equivalent for a value paid to the United States. The *Galphin* principal was paid under a late act of Congress—as a matter of grace, say some; but, at any rate, as a matter of discretion. *Alabama's* principal accrued under a treaty compact, and was paid as a *right*, without Congressional aid.

But the gravamen of the Galphin case was, that *Executive officers* paid interest without a special enactment by Congress. Its opponents do not allege that interest is not to be paid by the United States under any circumstances, or that *Congress* cannot order its payment; but they object to its unauthorized payment by Executive officers as an undue exercise of power.

It is *to Congress* Alabama comes and appeals for justice. She supplicates not for *favor*, but asks for *rights*—rights admitted, and long withheld; and she comes with clean hands. *Her* faith to the nation and to individuals is untarnished. She has never been behind her sister States in upbuilding and sustaining the institutions of our country; and, in the early policy of encouraging the sales of public lands, she has submitted to more sacrifices than any of the land States.

Would it comport with the dignity of a great nation to withhold justice in the present case? The United States demanded and received from Great Britain that justice in a similar case; they exact it from the States of the Union; they enforce it from their own citizens in all dealings with them. Is it consistent, is it *right*, that a rule should exist, *always* in *favor* of a nation, but *never* against her?

Are the great principles of justice to be powerless, when a nation is the subject of their application? And is this Union to protect itself behind the doctrine of the English crown, that "the King can do no wrong?"

Nay, rather let the contrary doctrine obtain; let justice be ever most inflexible, fair dealing most pure, and honor most scrupulous in the dealings of a nation, herself the asserter and the exemplar of an unswerving code of principles, as the only foundation on which a nation's *true* prosperity and glory can rest.

Respectfully submitted.

JEFF. F. JACKSON,
Agent for the State of Alabama.

WASHINGTON, *June* 25, 1850.

APPENDIX.

Exhibit A,

Showing the interest which the State of Alabama now claims. See the last column of Statement.

The following Statement exhibits the sums paid for lands in Alabama, with the dates when paid, but which were withheld from the fund account of the State until the restatement thereof—☞ALL THESE FACTS BEING TAKEN FROM THE OFFICIAL STATEMENT OF THE TREASURY, NOW OF RECORD THERE.☜

It also exhibits the State's per centage on these omitted payments; the period for which it was unpaid; and the interest thereon at 6 per cent.

ST. STEPHEN'S DISTRICT.

Period when sales were made.		Amount of purchase money paid in each quarter.	State's per centage thereon, 5 per cent.	Amount of interest at 6 per cent. on State's portion, from date when due to 30th June, 1850, and of 2d quarter.	
Year.	Quarter.			Period.	Amount.
				Yrs. mos.	
1821	3d qr., ending Sept. 30	$80,853 84	$4,042 69	28 9	$6,973 60
1822	3d " " Sept. 30	879 76	43 98	27 9	72 98
1823	3d " " Sept. 30	163 84	8 19	26 9	13 11
1824	3d " " Sept. 30	4,578 97	228 94	25 9	353 55
1824	4th " " Dec. 31	6,199 86	309 99	25 6	464 24
1825	1st " " March 31	49,553 11	2,477 65	25 3	3,753 41
1825	2d " " June 30	9,816 25	490 81	25 –	736 00
1826	4th " " Dec. 31	447 84	22 39	23 6	31 49
1827	1st " " March 31	610 49	30 52	23 3	42 55
1827	2d " " June 30	8,840 92	442 04	23 –	609 96
1827	3d " " Sept. 30	4,812 56	240 62	22 9	328 28
1828	3d " " Sept. 30	310 99	15 54	21 9	20 23
1829	1st " " March 31	1,449 10	72 45	21 3	92 44
1829	2d " " June 30	7,214 02	360 70	21 –	454 44
1829	3d " " Sept. 30	5,015 03	250 75	20 9	312 08
1831	1st " " March 31	689 87	34 49	19 3	39 65
1831	2d " " June 30	2,845 25	142 26	19 –	162 07
1831	3d " " Sept. 30	3,746 33	187 31	18 9	210 57
		$188,028 03			$14,670 65

STATEMENT—Continued.

CAHABA DISTRICT.

Year.	Quarter.	Amount of purchase money paid in each quarter.	State's per centage thereon, 5 per cent.	Amount of interest, at 6 per cent., on State's portion, from date when due to 30th June, 1850, end of 2d quarter. Period.	Amount.
				Yrs. mos.	
1821	3d qr., ending Sept. 30	$249,643 40	$12,482 17	28 9	$22,107 74
1822	3d " " Sept. 30	2,566 43	128 32	27 9	213 40
1823	3d " " Sept. 30	285 48	14 27	26 9	22 74
1825	3d " " Sept. 30	194,815 60	9,740 78	24 9	14,464 89
1827	2d " " June 30	60,404 78	3,020 23	23 -	4,167 83
1829	2d " " June 30	41,753 46	2,087 67	21 -	2,630 46
1831	1st " " March 31	3,638 31	181 91	19 3	210 01
1831	2d " " June 30	38,638 00	1,931 90	19 -	2,202 29
		$591,745 46			$46,019 36

HUNTSVILLE DISTRICT.

Year.	Quarter.	Amount of purchase money paid in each quarter.	State's per centage thereon, 5 per cent.	Period.	Amount.
1821	3d qr., ending Sept. 30	$658,489 25	$32,924 46	28 9	$56,794 48
1822	3d " " Sept. 30	4,179 43	208 97	27 9	347 71
1824	3d " " Sept. 30	280 18	14 00	25 9	21 63
1824	4th " " Dec. 31	1,078 27	53 91	25 6	82 36
1825	1st " " March 31	51,986 08	2,599 30	25 3	3,937 73
1825	2d " " June 30	20,773 99	1,038 69	25 -	1,558 00
1826	3d " " Sept. 30	9,077 43	453 87	23 9	646 71
1826	4th " " Dec. 31	3,695 42	184 77	23 6	260 38
1827	1st " " March 31	3,833 96	191 69	23 3	267 37
1827	2d " " June 30	30,326 48	1,516 32	23 -	2,092 31
1827	3d " " Sept. 30	41,315 44	2,065 77	22 9	2,819 64
1828	2d " " June 30	75	03	22 -	04
1828	3d " " Sept. 30	79 33	3 96	21 9	4 90
1828	4th " " Dec. 31	375 52	18 77	21 6	24 08
1829	1st " " March 31	3,431 93	171 59	21 3	218 66
1829	2d " " June 30	57,265 67	2,863 28	21 -	3,607 59
1829	3d " " Sept. 30	39,013 29	1 950 66	20 9	2,428 34
1830	4th " " Dec. 31	150,896 43	7,544 82	19 6	8,827 26
1831	1st " " March 31	16,395 70	819 78	19 3	946 71
1831	2d " " June 30	227,944 34	11,397 21	19 -	12,992 77
1831	3d " " Sept. 30	30,892 60	1,544 63	18 9	1,737 55
		$1,351,331 57			99,616 22
	St. Stephen's				14,670 65
	Cahaba				46,019 36
	Grand total				$160,306 23

Exhibit "B."

Schedule shewing the moneys overpaid to the United States by Alabama.

Total principal on which the United States charged interest from 1836 to present time - - -	$1,697,000 00
Deduct amount due at that time by the United States to Alabama, it being a good set-off to so much of the principal, but not endorsed on the bonds - - - - - - - - -	104,000 00
True amount of State indebtedness ☞ - -	1,593,000 00
And on which sum only Alabama ought to have paid interest.	
Amount of interest paid annually by the State, being 6 per cent. on $1,697,000 - - - -	$101,820 00
Amount of interest on $1,593,000, the *true* principal - - - - - - - - -	95,580 00
	$6,240 00
Difference between the true interest, and the am't paid - - - - - - - - - -	$6,240 00
This excess of interest, $6,240, was wrongfully paid by Alabama from July, 1836, to the present time in semi-annual payments. The following table exhibits the account thereof against the United States: on the usual principles of rectifying an erroneous payment of money.	

Exhibit "B"—Continued.

Date of overpayment.	Amount overpaid.	Interest at 6 p. ct. on amount overpaid from date of overpayment to July 1, 1850.	Period for which interest calculated.	
			Years.	Months.
1st July, 1836	$3,120 00	$2,620 80	14	–
1st Jan., 1837	3,120 00	2,527 20	13	6
1st July, 1837	3,120 00	2,433 60	13	–
1st Jan., 1838	3,120 00	2,340 00	12	6
1st July, 1838	3,120 00	2,246 40	12	–
1st Jan., 1839	3,120 00	2,152 80	11	6
1st July, 1839	3,120 00	2,059 20	11	–
1st Jan., 1840	3,120 00	1,965 60	10	6
1st July, 1840	3,120 00	1,872 00	10	–
1st Jan., 1841	3,120 00	1,778 40	9	6
1st July, 1841	3,120 00	1,684 80	9	–
1st Jan., 1842	3,120 00	1,591 20	8	6
1st July, 1842	3,120 00	1,497 60	8	–
1st Jan., 1843	3,120 00	1,404 00	7	6
1st July, 1843	3,120 00	1,310 40	7	–
1st Jan., 1844	3,120 00	1,216 80	6	6
1st July, 1844	3,120 00	1,123 20	6	–
1st Jan., 1845	3,120 00	1,029 60	5	6
1st July, 1845	3,120 00	936 00	5	–
1st Jan., 1846	3,120 00	842 40	4	6
1st July, 1846	3,120 00	748 80	4	–
1st Jan., 1847	3,120 00	655 20	3	6
1st July, 1847	3,120 00	561 60	3	–
1st Jan., 1848	3,120 00	468 00	2	6
1st July, 1848	3,120 00	374 40	2	–
1st Jan., 1849	3,120 00	280 80	1	6
1st July, 1849	3,120 00	187 20	1	–
1st Jan., 1850	3,120 00	93 60	0	6
Amount overpaid	87,360 00	$38,001 60		
Interest thereon -	38,001 60			
Total - -	$125,361 60			

Exhibit C.

Attorney General Wirt's letter to Mr. Meigs, Commissioner of the Land Office, 4th Nov., 1840, *page* 1387, *Att. General's opinions.*

This opinion refers to taxation in Illinois. It states the 5 years' exemption from tax of lands sold after 1st January, 1819; and that the State considered lands on which one-fourth of the purchase money had been paid, as subject to the exemption provision. He says: "The doubt is, whether the sale must not be consummated by the payment of the whole of the purchase money and the passing of the patent, before the lands can be said to be sold.

"If so, lands entered before the 1st January, 1819, and one-fourth of the purchase money paid on them, if standing in this predicament at that day, are still exempt from taxation, because the sale is not complete.

"If, however, the United States have recognised the liability of lands thus circumstanced to be taxed, by issuing patents to purchasers under the sale for taxes, there is an end of the question. Will you say what the practice is," &c.

Mr. Meigs replies as follows:

"It has been my opinion, that the lands sold by the United States in any territory prior to its admission into the Union, were exempt from taxes for 5 years from the time of sale. The lands were sold on a credit of 5 years, and if not paid for in that time, would revert to the United States. Under this opinion I certainly would not issue a patent to a purchaser at a tax sale, even if he tendered the balance due to the U. States, unless he produced an assignment from the original purchaser.

"I do not know that a single application has been made for a patent by a purchaser at a tax sale; if such application has been made, and a patent issued, it issued to him as assignee of the original purchaser on production of the assignment, and without any regard to the tax sale." Page. 15, Pub. Lands, vol. 2.

Exhibit D.

Mr. Taney to the Secretary of War, Sept. 10, 1831, *page* 841.

"I am not aware of any statute of the United States that forbids the Secretary of War, or the accounting officers, to allow interest to a claimant, if it should appear that interest is justly due to him. As the United States are always ready to pay, when a claim is presented, supported by proper vouchers, it can rarely, if ever, happen, that they are justly chargeable with interest, because it is the fault of the claimant, if he delays presenting his claim, or does not bring forward the proper vouchers to prove it, and justify its payment. But if in Major Tharp's case, or in any other, the Secretary of War, upon a review of the whole evidence, should be of opinion that interest is justly due to the claimant, I think he may legally allow it."

www.ingramcontent.com/pod-product-compliance
Lightning Source LLC
LaVergne TN
LVHW011133110826
845150LV00008B/2325

* 9 7 8 1 4 1 8 1 9 4 8 8 8 *